By rearranging the wheel layout of a tricycle, the forecar came into being, in which the passenger sat in a comfortable, upholstered seat. Unfortunately, the passenger also acted as a weather break for the rider and gained a grandstand view of any impending accident! Nonetheless, it represented a marked improvement over the trailer, despite its own shortcomings. Here it has even lulled the passenger to sleep, warning instrument at the ready. The machine is a 1903 Rex photographed in 1975.

VETERAN MOTORCYCLES

Jeff Clew

Shire Publications Ltd

CONTENTS

In the beginning 3

Hazards of the open road 9

Competition brings improvements 14

More power and greater refinement .. 20

The industry gets into its stride 25

Further reading and clubs 31

Places to visit 32

Published in 1995 by Shire Publications Ltd, Cromwell House, Church Street, Princes Risborough, Buckinghamshire HP27 9AA, UK.
Copyright © 1995 by Jeff Clew. First edition 1995. Shire Album 313. ISBN 0 7478 0276 9. Jeff Clew is hereby identified as the author of this work in accordance with Section 77 of the Copyright, Designs and Patents Act 1988. All rights reserved. No part of this publication may be reproduced or transmitted in any form or by any means, electronic or mechanical, including photocopy, recording, or any information storage and retrieval system, without permission in writing from the publishers.

Printed in Great Britain by CIT Printing Services, Press Buildings, Merlins Bridge, Haverfordwest, Dyfed SA61 1XF.

British Library Cataloguing in Publication Data: Clew, Jeff. Veteran Motorcycles. – (Shire Albums; No. 313). I. Title II. Series. 629.227509. ISBN 0-7478-0276-9.

Editorial Consultant: Michael E. Ware, Curator of the National Motor Museum, Beaulieu, Hampshire.

ACKNOWLEDGEMENTS
My grateful thanks to Geoff Morris, a former Pioneer Machine Registrar for the Sunbeam Motor Cycle Club, who kindly read my manuscript and made a number of useful suggestions about its content. My thanks also to the Photographic Library of the National Motor Museum at Beaulieu, who allowed me to select and use photographs from their archive. Photographs are reproduced by kind permission of the National Motor Museum.

Cover: *A 3¹/₂ horsepower 1912 Favourite-AKD, owned by Peter Hallowes of Sturminster Newton, Dorset.*

A notable event occurred in 1907 when Teddy Hastings brought his 4 horsepower Indian twin from America to ride in the ACC's 1000 mile (1600 km) trial. He put up an amazing performance, to score 994 out of a possible 1000 marks, the resultant publicity making a great deal of impact on British motorcyclists. Seen in the photograph with Hastings are left to right: George Reynolds (timekeeper), J. W. G. Brooker and Billy Wells, who was then riding for Vindec but later represented Indian interests in Britain.

The Hildebrand and Wolfmüller of 1894 seems to have prior claim to have been the first workable motorcycle. Its 'open' metal tube frame housed a water-cooled twin-cylinder four-stroke engine of 1489 cc, which followed locomotive practice in having long connecting rods directly attached to cranks on the rear wheel. As there was no flywheel to sustain inertia, external rubber straps were fitted to help return the pistons on their upward strokes.

IN THE BEGINNING

No one can be sure who made the first motorcycle, although most probably it was the Hildebrand brothers, Heinrich and Wilhelm, who, assisted by Alois Wolfmüller, had a machine on the road in 1884. Gottlieb Daimler and Wilhelm Maybach also had a workable engine that year, but it was not until 1885 that a more refined version was fitted into a crude bicycle.

The Hildebrand and Wolfmuller was the more ambitious of the two German designs. It was based on a twin-cylinder four-stroke engine of 1489 cc, mounted at an angle in an 'open' frame of four inclined tubes, with conventional handlebars, wheels and a saddle. It was water-cooled, the rear mudguard acting as a reservoir. The drive to the rear wheel followed locomotive practice, long connecting rods being attached to cranks on the rear wheel, the hub containing an epicyclic reduction gear. With no internal flywheel to sustain momentum, rubber straps helped to return the pistons on their upward strokes. It was alleged to be capable of 24 mph (39 km/h).

Plans were made for its large-scale production, with a licensing agreement for its manufacture in France. Unfortunately, they were short-lived when limitations in the design became evident. The lack of a flywheel meant the engine ran unevenly, and the hot-tube ignition was unreliable. Instead, the company went into liquidation.

The 264 cc capacity single-cylinder four-stroke engine designed by Daimler and Maybach in 1894 was the true forerunner of the internal combustion engine we know today. It had a crankcase containing two flywheels, one either side of the crankpin, and an inlet over exhaust valve layout, the inlet valve being of the atmospheric type, the exhaust operated mechanically by a cam. A power-driven fan kept the engine at the correct temperature in the absence of any cooling fins. The carburettor was float-controlled and the ignition hot-tube.

In 1895 the engine was mounted vertically in a crudely made wooden 'boneshaker' bicycle. The rider sat high

3

Daimler and Maybach had a 264 cc single-cylinder four-stroke engine in 1894, and a complete motorcycle a year later. Their engine can be regarded as the true forerunner of the internal combustion engine as we know it today. It was mounted in a crude wooden frame with wooden wheels, reminiscent of a 'hobby horse' bicycle. Having the saddle immediately above the engine proved an unsatisfactory arrangement, as some found to their cost.

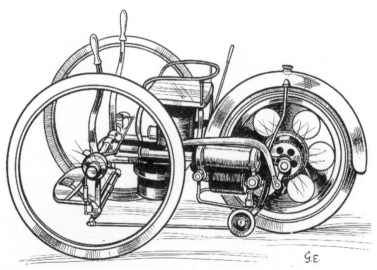

Edward Butler, an engineer from Erith, Kent, patented a design for a two-stroke motor tricycle in 1894, but handicapped by the Road Acts of 1861 and 1865 and a lack of investors it did not become a reality until four years later. By then he had decided to design and use his own four-stroke engine. This engine embodied a number of advanced features, which included a spray carburettor, coil ignition and a distributor.

4

De Dion Bouton were amongst the first to achieve commercial success after one of their motor tricycles had won the Paris-Marseilles-Paris race of 1896. The single-cylinder four-stroke engine was mounted behind the rear wheels, which it drove through a differential. By 1899 the engine capacity had been increased to $1^3/4$ horsepower and the Motor Manufacturing Company took out a licence to make the De Dion tricycle in Coventry with an engine uprated to $2^1/4$ horsepower.

up on a saddle directly above the engine, which necessitated fitting additional small stabiliser wheels. Drive was by belt to a countershaft and thence by pinion to an internally toothed ring on the rear wheel. Daimler's son Paúl carried out the testing and on one $7^1/2$ mile (12 km/h) journey had to abandon the machine when the saddle caught fire! The *Einspur* 'single track', as it was called, progressed no further after its inventors became more interested in making a car engine.

In Britain Edward Butler had patented a design for a motor tricycle in 1894, but had been severely handicapped by the Road Acts of 1861 and 1865. They restricted any mechanically propelled vehicle to 4 mph (6 km/h) and to 2 mph (3 km/h) in towns, and required that it was preceded by a person on foot carrying a red flag. When these acts were replaced by the Locomotives on Highways Act of 1896, Butler and the other British inventors had the freedom they desired. Yet it was not until the turn of the century that motor-

cycles began to appear, as attention was at first directed toward motor tricycles.

By far the most popular tricycle was the French De Dion Bouton, the engine of which drove the differential rear axle by exposed spur gear pinions. A licensing agreement permitted it to be made in Britain by H. J. Lawson's Motor Manufacturing Company of Coventry. Such was its success that other British manufacturers, such as Ariel, Enfield and Swift, began to design and make tricycles powered by their own engines.

The tricycle had its limitations though, especially if the engine was mounted behind the rear axle (as the De Dion Bouton), which made it unbalanced. The exposed driving gears created problems too, as they were noisy and easily damaged. These and other problems, accentuated by the need to carry a passenger, suggested rearranging the layout so that the location of the wheels was transposed. By having the twin wheels at the front, a seat could be placed between them, converting the

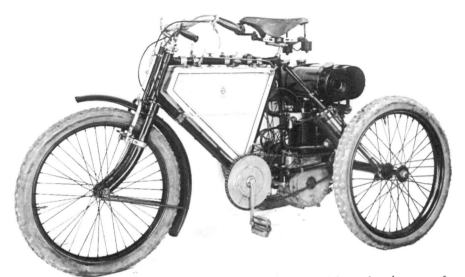

Ariel, one of Britain's oldest motorcycle manufacturers, were quick to take advantage of a basic flaw in the De Dion Bouton design. Although Ariel used a De Dion engine in their own motor tricycle, they mounted it forward of the rear axle, where its weight was better balanced and the stability of the tricycle improved. Later, a water-cooled cylinder head was introduced, so that the rear-mounted engine was less likely to overheat.

All manner of locations were tried for the installation of an engine in a motorcycle frame, but none more ingenious than this 200 cc Perks and Birch 'Motor-Wheel'. The aluminium alloy wheel contained not only the engine unit that drove the wheel hub through a reduction gear, but also the petrol tank. It is seen here fitted to a 1901 Singer tricycle, being a direct replacement for the original front wheel. It could also be fitted in place of the rear wheel of a pedal cycle.

6

The 'clip on' type of engine was also favoured by many manufacturers, including Triumph, who used this $2^1/4$ horsepower Belgian-made Minerva engine for their first model in 1902. They also tried a 293 cc British-made JAP engine, mounted in a similar manner, before they designed and made their own engine in 1905. They were the first to use an all ball-bearing engine.

Colonel Holden upheld British prestige by designing and making the first four-cylinder motorcycle. The engine unit was a horizontally mounted water-cooled flat four which, like the Hildebrand and Wolfmuller, drove a small-diameter rear wheel by long connecting rods and cranks. Although without a flywheel, the engine ran sufficiently smoothly to take any harshness out of the drive. At only 400 rpm it was capable of propelling the machine at 24 mph (39km/h). It was marketed from 1899 to 1902.

The best position for an engine was finally determined by the Werner brothers, who made both engines and complete motorcycles in Paris. In 1901 they located it in the position normally occupied by the bottom bracket of a pedal cycle. Apart from providing a low centre of gravity, the crankcase of the engine became a structural part of the frame. Other manufacturers soon followed suit; the Werner brothers had established a precedent that is still followed today.

motor tricycle into a forecar. The hapless passenger unwittingly acted as a weather break for the driver and had a grandstand view of any impending accident!

When motorcycles began to appear around 1900, each manufacturer had his own idea where the engine should be. Royal Enfield and Raleigh had it over the front wheel. Minerva and many others had it clipped to the front down tube, Singer inside the rear wheel, Ormonde under the saddle and the Shaw between the bottom bracket and the rear wheel. Colonel Holden designed and built his own version of the Hildebrand and Wolfmuller, and had the honour of making Britain's first four-cylinder motorcycle.

The answer came in 1901 when Werner Frères, of Paris, located their engine in the bottom bracket position, adding an additional horizontal strengthening tube below the petrol tank. It provided the ideal solution to the problem – the diamond frame, still in use today.

The need to carry a passenger, usually the rider's girlfriend or wife, led to tow-ing a trailer with an upholstered seat. Unfortunately the passenger collected not only all the dust, road debris and horse droppings disturbed by the machine, but also the oil discharged by the machine's exhaust. Sometimes a trailer connection would break without the rider knowing, causing it to flip over backwards and dump its distraught passenger in a most ungraceful manner! The trailer was soon replaced by the sidecar.

No description of the early days would be complete without mention of E. J. Pennington, an extrovert American. His machines had two horizontal and uncooled cylinders mounted behind the rear wheel, which they drove by short cranks. He claimed they would run on paraffin due to the 'long mingling spark' of his ignition system and were suitable for cross-country work, where they could be jumped across rivers! His extravagant claims brought in large orders, netting him something in the region of £100,000 before his exposure as a charlatan. Not one Pennington motorcycle was ever sold.

As soon as motorcycles became powerful enough, various means were devised for carrying a passenger. Ariel came up with this ingenious idea of adapting a pedal cycle so that it could be attached to the rear of their tricycle. It was not very practical, as the passenger collected all the dust, mud and other debris disturbed by the rear wheels, as well as the fumes and oil discharged by the exhaust. Many a promising romance ended abruptly after a ride on a trailer!

HAZARDS OF THE OPEN ROAD

In the early 1900s any ride on a motorcycle was a voyage of adventure. Before wheeling the machine out of its shed or garage, it was first necessary to carry out a number of checks. As there were no filling stations, petrol had to be ordered in advance, so the first check was to ensure the tank contained enough petrol to take the rider to and from the intended destination. Next came an oil check, then a further check to see if the battery had held its charge. It was wise also to make sure none of the wiring was beginning to chafe through. A quick look at the drive belt was in order, to be sure the fastener that joined the two ends had not started to pull through. Anything that was likely to cause an involuntary roadside stop was worthy of attention.

It was then necessary to find whether the engine was 'free', so that it could be turned over easily by the pedals whilst the machine was on its stand. Oils in those days were gummy when cold, and as a cast-iron piston is run with less clearance in a cylinder barrel than an alloy one, it would sometimes prove almost immovable. To free it, paraffin had to be dribbled into the cylinder through a tap in its top, and the engine rotated by the pedals after it had been closed. Once the engine was free, the controls had then to be set in what seemed to be the best position for starting, and the ignition switched on. If the rider was lucky, it would start after more vigorous pedalling and could be allowed to warm up.

As the drive was direct to the rear wheel and there was no clutch, the engine had to be stopped before the machine could be taken off its stand and ridden on the road. The rider, now in full riding clothing, had to pedal it off and keep pedalling until the engine would run under its own power. It was a decided advantage to be strong, fit and of athletic build.

Constant juggling of the controls was essential to keep the machine in motion, especially if it had a surface carburettor. Every pothole in the road (and there were plenty of them!) upset the carburation and constantly changed the mixture strength. A squirt of oil to the engine had to be given by a hand-operated pump every few miles and, when a hill came into sight, the rider had to take a fast run at it before resorting to more furious pedalling to help it get to the top, or dismounting and running alongside. If it was raining or the road was wet, not only was belt slip in-

9

Whereas the Werner brothers had used the crankcase to form a structural part of a motorcycle frame, Humber used the entire engine to replace the front down tube by inclining it forward. Here it is seen as a structural part of their 1903 forecar. It became a characteristic adopted in later years by Phelon and Moore, who made Panther motorcycles at Cleckheaton in West Yorkshire.

evitable, but, the motorcycle being top-heavy, it could also sideslip and unseat its rider.

The inadequacy of the lamps then available made night riding hazardous. The early oil lamps gave a feeble light and soon shook to pieces. Acetylene lights were better, but only if the whole system was kept clean, the carbide container recharged regularly, and the water reservoir topped up. The gas was generated by dripping water on to lumps of calcium carbide.

Punctures were commonplace, as the roads were littered with debris, such as sharp fragments of horseshoes or nails from them. The next most frequent cause for a roadside halt was when a belt fastener pulled through, the belt often administering the rider a hefty thwack on the behind as it broke. It was a filthy job

to repair it as the belt was invariably soaked in engine oil and slush from the road. As there were no roadside garages or repairers, it paid dividends to carry a comprehensive repair kit, including a large adjustable spanner to bend the pedals back into shape if they were bent in a fall. Starting without being able to use them was not possible.

If all else failed, a local blacksmith was the last hope. Few had even rudimentary knowledge of the internal combustion engine, and carried no spares, so the now desperate rider was very much at their mercy. Many brought their defunct motorcycles back by horse and cart.

Frequent brushes with the law were not uncommon. The police readily summonsed motorcyclists for excessive speed or noise. When they appeared in court they were not looked upon favourably by

A number of motorcar manufacturers built their own forecars around 1900, including Riley and Lagonda. This 4 horsepower 1905 example was made by Rover and catalogued as their New Suspended Tri-Car. The seat occupied by the passenger is mounted on leaf springs and there is some protection for the feet as well as an apron to help ward off rain and the cold, but it is doubtful whether the radiator to the rear was of much help.

Although the motorcycle was still in its early stages of development, some beneficial improvements were already taking shape. The state of the unmade roads soon made it evident that an unsprung front fork like that fitted to the average pedal cycle was totally unsuitable. Without modifying the single-strut fork, Ariel devised this spring link arrangement for the front wheel on their 1903 model. This is alleged to be a 1903 model, but the forward mounted magneto would seem to make this dating questionable.

Early sporting events, such as hill climbs, were held mostly on the Continent, as seen here with the militiaman and his fixed bayonet on the left. With no fire extinguisher in sight, the rider and a spectator try valiantly to blow out the fire that has caused the former to dismount. The onlooker smoking a cigarette is not being particularly helpful.

The Quadrant tends to be a forgotten make, even though the company continued to make motorcycles until 1928. Another of the pioneers of motorcycle manufacture in Britain, Quadrant made a major contribution by simplifying the arrangement of the many separate controls, so that one lever would serve several functions. Tom Silver will always be associated with Quadrant for his early attempts on the Land's End to John O'Groats record.

Although riding a motorcycle was considered to be undignified and most unladylike in the early days, this did not deter some ladies from riding their own machines. Soon there were enough of them for ladies' models to be included in a manufacturer's catalogue, the main feature being a 'dropped' frame that allowed the machine to be ridden whilst wearing a skirt. The ladies took great pride in their appearance, as exemplified in this photograph of an unknown lady riding a Ladies' Model Douglas twin.

magistrates, most of whom were horse lovers who expressed their dislike of motorcyclists by hefty fines.

It may be wondered why anyone bothered to ride a motorcycle at all. As with anything new, it was the spirit of adventure that was the driving factor, and the acknowledgement that, although there were irritating teething problems, it would soon be possible to sort them out. Motorcycle clubs helped bring together fellow enthusiasts, aided by the publication of two indispensable weekly magazines, *Motor Cycling* and *The Motor Cycle*.

Motorcycling attracted quite a few ladies, who enjoyed riding for riding's sake, on an an 'open' frame model which could be ridden whilst wearing a skirt. Amongst the more notable lady riders were Muriel Hind, who contributed a regular column to *Motor Cycling* aimed at encouraging women to take part in this new pastime, and Rosa Hammett. Rosa thought nothing of a 100 mile (160 km) ride and claimed a ride of twelve hours duration was well within a woman's capabilities. Both rode in competition events.

The vertical twin is regarded as a relatively recent engine development, which was capitalised upon by Edward Turner of the Triumph Engineering Company in 1937. It will come as a surprise to many that in 1905 a Belgian manufacturer produced this 616 cc side-valve vertical twin, which had a three-bearing crankshaft and mechanically operated valves.

COMPETITION BRINGS IMPROVEMENTS

By around 1905, the motorcycle had begun to shake off its frail and temperamental image. The spray carburettor had superseded its crude surface-type predecessor, and a further step forward came with the introduction of the high-tension magneto. Able to generate its own spark, it required neither battery nor coil. The elimination of these two problem areas made the motorcycle more dependable. The Motor Car Act of 1903 required all motor vehicles to be registered and carry registration plates at the front and rear, from 1st January 1904. By the end of that year, 26,906 motorcycles had been registered.

There was now a tendency to have both valves mechanically operated. Still favoured by some, the automatic inlet valve restricted an engine's performance. Fitted with a light return spring, it was sucked open when the piston descended on the induction stroke. As engine speeds began to rise, it was no longer able to keep pace. Variable speed gears had also begun to appear, with some form of disconnecting

the drive to the rear wheel.

British-made motorcycles were now more evident, with fewer of foreign manufacture to be seen. Some makers, who had previously fitted engines of continental manufacture, were fitting their own. The industry was grouped around Birmingham and Coventry, where the largest pool of engineering talent lay, although there were other successful manufacturers elsewhere including Matchless and BAT in London, P & M in Yorkshire, Dot in Manchester and, from 1907, Douglas in Bristol.

With so many different makes on the market, manufacturers needed to show their own machines were better than those of any other. The obvious answer was to pit them against their rivals in open competition and make capital out of their successes. To do so in road races was difficult, because it was only on the Continent that public highways could be used. Their organisers were also inclined to interpret the regulations more liberally in favour of their own countrymen. Road racing in Britain had to take place at off-road ven-

14

Manufacturers gained early publicity by sponsoring riders to break the record for the time taken to ride from Land's End to John O'Groats non-stop. Here are two such contestants with their 1904 Rex singles on arrival at John O'Groats, a distance of approximately 900 miles (1450 km). It was by no means an easy task just to get there, let alone to do so in record time, because of the state of the roads at that time. Eventually these attempts were prohibited as they were putting pedestrians, other road users, and the riders themselves at risk.

The Auto Cycle Club (later to become the Auto Cycle Union) took on the organisation of motorcycling events in Britain after being founded in 1908 as a branch of the RAC. The aims were to protect the interests of motorcyclists and to encourage the sport and pastime of motorcycling. From 1924 onwards they existed solely for encouraging and controlling motorcycle sport. Seen here is the start of an ACC Quarterly Trial from the yard of the Chequers at Uxbridge, Middlesex.

Motorcycle racing on public roads in the British Isles began in 1907. The first Tourist Trophy Races took place in the Isle of Man. A 15.8 mile (25.4 km) course was used initially, starting and finishing at St John's. Two separate classes were run, one for twin-cylinder machines and one for singles. This historic photograph shows the start of the 1907 single-cylinder class.

ues such as the cycle pacing track at Canning Town, east London.

Long-distance endurance feats had their appeal, especially timed 'End to End' runs, from John O'Groats to Land's End. They were soon discouraged by the Auto-Cycle Union, the body that controlled motorcycle sport in Britain, as riders were putting themselves, and the general public, at risk.

Attention was then directed towards marathon-like events such as the A-CU's

Six Days Trial or the Scottish Six Days Trial (which commenced as a five-days trial in 1909). An outright win in any of these made good advertising copy and could bring the machine's manufacturer overnight success.

Problems arising from long-distance road racing on the Continent were overcome by using the public highways in the Isle of Man, where there were no restrictions on their use. The first Tourist Trophy Races were held there towards the

The Twin Cylinder Class of the 1907 TT was won by Rem Fowler riding a Norton powered by a Peugeot vee-twin engine. This photograph was taken during the Golden Jubilee of the TT in 1957, when he posed with this replica of the Norton he rode to victory in 1907. His winning race average speed was 36.22 mph (58.3 km/h), a considerable achievement when some riders had to dismount on hills and run alongside their machines to keep them going.

The opening of Brooklands at Weybridge, Surrey, in 1907 gave further encouragement to the British motorcycle and motorcar manufacturers. Now they had access to a purpose-built high-speed test track and no longer needed to use the public highway. The track was steeply banked and there was always fear of going over the top. Reuben Harveyson was one of a few who did that on his Indian vee-twin. He was fortunate to escape almost unscathed.

end of May 1907, for which only machines similar to those sold to the public would be eligible. With the start at St John's, the 15.8 mile (25.4 km) course ran through Ballacraine, Kirkmichael and Peel, before returning to St John's. It had to be lapped ten times, with a compulsory ten-minute stop after the first five laps had been completed. The TT had been born, to continue right up to the present day.

1907 was a memorable year in another respect. A wealthy landowner in Surrey, H. F. Locke-King, was saddened that the development of the car

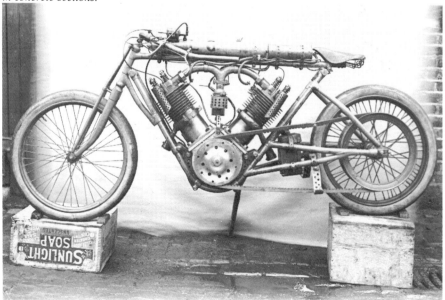

Racing at Brooklands encouraged the appearance of some freak machines, such as this NLG powered by a massive 2714 cc 90 vee-twin JAP engine designed for use in an aircraft. The NLG must have proved very uncomfortable to ride and quite difficult to handle, as it is devoid of springing, front and rear. Brooklands had a notoriously bumpy surface as it had been laid in concrete sections.

Inter-Varsity Challenge Races were staged at Brooklands, such as this meeting between Oxford and Cambridge universities. The machine in the foreground deserves attention as it has a Truffault front fork, a later version of which became very popular in the 1950s as the Earles fork.

Perhaps because the race was run over closed public roads, there was no compulsion to wear protective clothing as this shot taken in Peel during the 1908 TT clearly shows. Riding in his shirt sleeves and using his goggles to retain his cloth cap, H. Lister Cooper (3 ½ horsepower Triumph) leads E. G. Young (3½ horsepower Acme) in the Single Cylinder Class. Lister-Cooper finished seventh but Young was forced to retire for undisclosed reasons.

Hill climbs remained very popular events as they are easy to arrange once a sufficiently challenging hill with a relatively smooth surface has been found. Here a group of riders have staged an impromptu event at Ramsey Hairpin, possibly after having used a small section of the 37³/₄ mile (60.75 km) Mountain Course that first came into use during 1911. Even modern TT riders regard Ramsey Hairpin, with its acute left-hand bend, as a bottom-gear corner.

and motorcycle in Britain had been handicapped by having nowhere where vehicles could be tested at high speed. To remedy this, he had built, at his own expense, a high-speed track, steeply banked in places, on his estate at Weybridge. It was built in eight months after the ground had been cleared, a remarkable achievement, considering that no one had previous experience of laying a concrete surface on such a vast scale. Given the name Brooklands, the track was officially opened on 17th June 1907, to become the mecca for car and motorcycle racing until its closure at the outbreak of the Second World War.

Alfred Scott had designed a twin-cylinder two-stroke engine in 1904 and by 1908 was able to offer a complete motorcycle, the first six of which were made by the Jowett brothers of Bradford. When they began making their own car in 1909, Scott set up his own company in nearby Shipley to manufacture the motorcycle that bore his name. Of advanced design, it was fitted with his own two-speed gear and had a triangulated frame built from straight tubes. It set an entirely new standard in road holding and performance, to make the Scott one of motorcycling's most cherished names.

Not every motorcycle manufacturer had the capital and facilities to design and manufacture its own engine. The alternative was to buy in an engine of proprietary manufacture from a major supplier such as J. A. Prestwich and Company Ltd, of Tottenham, North London. This firm had been making engines since 1903 and could offer a range of good-quality singles and vee-twins. Rivalled only by F. E. Baker, who made Precision engines, JAP were Britain's largest engine manufacturer and renowned worldwide.

19

Pierce Arrow of Buffalo, New York, used the frame tubes of their motorcycles to carry the petrol and oil, and on their four-cylinder models the shaft drive to the rear wheel. This machine was discovered in Suffolk, formerly owned by a Pierce Arrow representative. The make was not very well-known in Britain and was often referred to colloquially as the 'Fierce Sparrow'!

MORE POWER AND GREATER REFINEMENT

The British motorcycle industry was in the doldrums from 1906 to 1909, new registrations falling to a low of just over eight thousand in 1907, against a total of 34,664 motorcycles in use. Confidence had been undermined by a rash of new manufacturers cashing in on the motorcycle's popularity with machines of dubious quality, yet the Triumph Cycle Company Ltd had continued to prosper. They had been fitting their own ball-bearing engine since 1905 and in 1907 filed a patent on a clutch within a rear wheel hub. An engine could now be started and the machine ridden off without using the pedals or a run and jump. The 'trusty' Triumph gained an enviable reputation for its reliability, to become a byword in the trade. Their yearly production rose from one thousand in 1907 to three thousand in 1909.

Motorcycle sales began to pick up by 1910, with almost two thousand more machines in use by the end of that year.

During the summer two legendary names joined the ranks of the manufacturers: BSA and Rudge. The former had been making motorcycle frames and cycle parts for some years, but not until now a complete machine.

In 1911 prospects were even more promising, when another newcomer, AJS, joined the fray. During the year Alfred Scott introduced the kickstarter, a far more convenient way of starting an engine.

The event to have most impact on the industry was the 1911 Isle of Man TT, run over the much longer 37¾ mile (60.75 km) Mountain Course, the long climb over Snaefell necessitating a variable-speed gear. Some, such as Zenith, had their own ingenious design, whilst others, such as the Phillipson, opted for adjustable engine pulleys. NSU had a combined epicyclic gear and engine pulley, and Scott and P & M their own tried and proven two-speed gears.

Four Indian vee-twins entered for the Senior Race provided a strong challenge

20

The sidecar superseded the trailer and the forecar as a better means of carrying a passenger in reasonable comfort, though often not providing adequate protection from the elements. Early sidecars with wickerwork bodies came into this category, their advantage being lightness in weight. It is unusual to come across a commercial sidecar with a wickerwork body, although some were probably used by the Post Office to carry parcels.

The Bradbury from Oldham, Lancashire, was a well-made machine. This 1910 model has an unusual feature – a crankcase that is an integral part of the frame. It was the idea of Mr Perks, who had been involved with the Perks and Birch Motor-Wheel. The Bradbury was made from 1902 to 1925 and was regarded with such respect that its loss to the industry was felt when production came to an end.

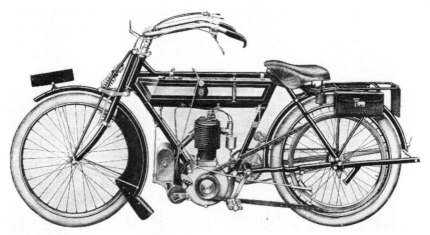

Although BSA had been making pedal cycles and motorcycle parts such as frames and forks, it was not until 1910 that they made their first complete motorcycle. It was fitted with a double-acting spring front fork, as shown here, and an engine having the classic 85 by 88 mm bore and stroke dimensions to give a 499 cc capacity. The BSA was made in the company's Redditch factory.

from the United States. They took the first three places (the fourth rider was disqualified for receiving unauthorised assistance) and it did not pass unnoticed that they were fitted with a two-speed countershaft gearbox and all-chain drive. A Scott had set up the lap record, before it was forced to retire. It too had all-chain drive.

The advantage of a countershaft gearbox was becoming obvious. Not only did it permit a wider range of gear ratios, but it was also more robust and easier to dis-

In Wolverhampton, the Stevens family had a similar interest in development through racing, using their own AJS machines which were fitted with their own single-cylinder engine. This photograph, showing A. J. Stevens on the left and J. D. Corke on the right, was taken during the 1911 TT. Three years later, the AJS made its mark, taking first and second places in the Junior Race.

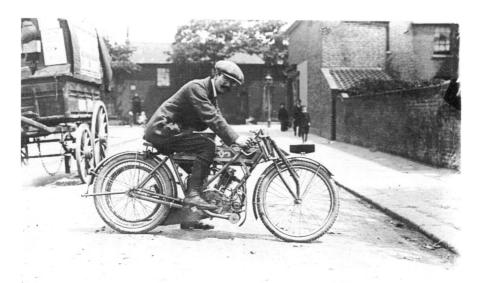

At Woolwich, London, Matchless were building vee-twins with a JAP engine that were successful in racing. Harry (seen here) and Charlie, two of the sons of Henry Collier, who owned the business, did most of the racing, assisted by Bert Colver. After the American Indian factory had scored an impressive win in the 1911 Senior TT, a match race was staged between a Matchless and an Indian. The Indian won in circumstances that were inconclusive.

mantle and repair. It could accommodate a better-located kickstarter than that in Scott's design. When Douglas copied the Indian gearbox design in 1910 and used it on the works-entered machines in that year's Scottish Six Days Trial, they won the Team Prize. The orders that followed put Douglas on a firm footing.

In 1912 the Sunbeam, the 'Gentleman's Motorcycle', built to a very high standard and with a finish second to none, made its debut. Also new was the very advanced 2½ horsepower Veloce, an inlet over exhaust four-

Alfred Scott, a quiet, unassuming genius from Bradford, changed the somewhat crude two-stroke engine out of all recognition. His first twin-cylinder design was patented in 1904 and by 1908 six prototype designs had been made by the Jowett brothers. Thereafter Scott formed his own production company to make them himself. Performance was such that a Scott broke the lap record in the 1911 Senior TT and won the race outright in 1912 and 1913. The rider is Frank Philipp, who finished eleventh in 1912.

stroke built in-unit with a two-speed gearbox and mechanical lubrication. It was too advanced for its day and few bought it. Veloce had instead to fall back on their standard model, a close copy of the 3½ horsepower Triumph.

Four-stroke motorcycle engines were almost all of the side-valve type, although JAP had produced an overhead-valve engine as far back as 1903. The development of the more efficient overhead-valve engine had been hindered by a lack of metallurgical knowledge. The key to the development of this type of engine lay in finding a suitable valve material to withstand the intense heat, without risk of failure. When a valve head broke off, it fell into the engine, to cause serious damage. In the side-valve design valve breakages were of lesser consequence, because the valve was at the side of the cylinder bore, head uppermost. If one broke, it was easy to remove and replace, if needs be by the roadside.

Alfred Scott had led the way in two-stroke design by experimenting with rotary induction valves with such success that one of these machines won the Senior TT in 1912 and 1913. Single-cylinder designs began to evolve from about 1912 onwards. All relied on a deflector piston, to minimise the escape of the incoming mixture through the exhaust port. The two-stroke's disadvantage was its reluctance to idle evenly at low speed.

Most engines were either singles or vee-twins, although Douglas remained faithful to the horizontally-opposed flat twin. A few in-line fours had been made, but they were expensive and sold only in small numbers. The Belgian FN proved the most successful, with the added attraction of having shaft final drive. The non-British machines that sold best were the Indian, from the United States, and the NSU, from Germany.

Arguments about whether chain or belt was the better method of drive continued, but it was the chain that won in the end. It took a long time, for the belt did not disappear completely until the mid 1920s.

P & M, who favoured the inclined engine layout pioneered by Humber, sued the Scott Engineering Company Ltd, whom they considered had infringed their clutchless two-speed gear design. The outcome was inconclusive as Scott continued with their own design throughout the vintage era. The Scott used a foot-operated pedal to change gear whereas the P & M had a hand lever, as illustrated.

John Wooler was always one for the unconventional and his Wooler motorcycle was no exception. Apart from its novel front and rear plunger-type suspension, this 344 cc model of 1912 had a horizontally opposed twin-cylinder engine. Finished in yellow and black, the Wooler was known thereafter as the 'Flying Banana'.

THE INDUSTRY GETS INTO ITS STRIDE

By the end of 1913 the popularity of the motorcycle had increased to such an extent that there were 97,784 in use in Britain, a figure that rose still higher to 128,678 by the end of 1914. Within a span of little more than five years the motorcycle had become a thoroughly reliable, go anywhere machine. Lessons learnt from competition in long-distance events and from racing in the Isle of Man had been put into practice, so that the average rider and the person who rode in competitions benefited alike. For most, a change to the countershaft type of gearbox, with its obvious benefits, had yet to come about, as it meant redesigning the frame. Their salvation came in the form of a compromise when Armstrong, and then Sturmey Archer, made available a three-speed hub gear. It fitted in place of the standard rear wheel, an added advantage being that it also contained a foot-operated free engine clutch. Its disadvantages were added weight at the rear and the restricted range of gear ratios. It did not lend itself to the fitting of a kickstarter either.

Some manufacturers, such as Matchless and Rudge, took advantage of another compromise, in the constant search for better performance. With one notable exception, overhead valves were still regarded with caution, but it was feasible to use an inlet over exhaust arrangement, in which the inlet valve was overhead and the exhaust valve in the customary side-valve position. Because the inlet valve ran cooler, the risk of it breaking and wrecking the engine was greatly reduced.

Douglas were one of the last to remain faithful to the antiquated and somewhat restrictive automatic inlet valve. They did not have both valves mechanically operated until 1912 – and reaped the benefit when Harry Bashall won that year's Junior TT for them. AJS had the courage to persevere with all-chain drive and seemed to have solved the problem by finishing first,

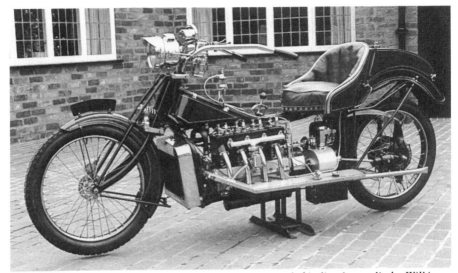

Another quite remarkable machine was the 848 cc water-cooled in-line four-cylinder Wilkinson TMC, a 1912 model of which is depicted here. It was made in Wilkinson Sword's factory in Chiswick and continued to be made until 1916, latterly by the Ogston Motor Company of Acton after Wilkinson became occupied with work resulting from the First World War. This machine was fully restored for display in the National Motorcycle Museum.

second, fourth and sixth in the 1914 Junior TT, although they had the advantage of four speeds too, by combining a two-speed gear with a two-speed countershaft. Douglas had used a similar four-speed gear arrangement on one of their 'works' entries in the 1912 TT, but it had failed to finish.

The single-cylinder two-stroke came into its own around 1913, even Triumph adding a 225 cc 'Baby' model to their range by the end of the year. Not having had a great deal of success with their four-stroke models, Veloce decided to manufacture their own two-stroke, using the name Velocette. With its two-speed gear and separate lubrication it proved such a success that the company forsook the manufacture of four-strokes until 1925 and had to continue using the Velocette trademark.

Motorcycling had become very popular in the United States too, with a wide variety of different makes, both singles and vee-twins. The latter were the more popular, with Indian and Harley-Davidson having the larger share of the market. Some of them had leaf-spring frames, as American

motorcyclists were accustomed to travelling longer distances on dirt roads, where the added comfort was an advantage. Many had experimented with spring frames or other means of isolating the rider from road shocks in Britain too, but the idea never seemed to appeal to many.

A number of interesting new designs first appeared in 1914, such as a 500 cc Douglas and a new horizontally opposed twin made by ABC. The Brough, made by George Brough's father, was another that followed a similar route, with a 496 cc overhead-valve engine. Triumph, meanwhile, had built a 650 cc side-valve vertical twin engine, the crankshaft of which allowed the pistons to rise and fall alternately and was fitted with a heavy external flywheel.

Sunbeam had a vee-twin in their range, fitted with a 770 cc JAP engine, whilst Charles Marston, the oldest son of John Marston (Sunbeam's founder), was making Villiers two-stroke engines in Villiers Street, Wolverhampton. The first Villiers engine, a unit-construction 349 cc four-

Most manufacturers now considered some form of variable gear essential, using either a Sturmey Archer or an Armstrong epicyclic three-speed gear (and clutch) in the rear wheel hub. Rudge went one better and had a Multi variable gear which gave a choice of ratios from $3^1/_2$ to $7^1/_2$ to 1. The rider of this 1914 TT entry is Manxman Tom Sheard, who won the Senior TT on a Douglas in 1923.

Record breaking was another activity that took place at Brooklands, much to the annoyance of local residents who often had to tolerate noise throughout the night. Jack Emerson, seen here sitting on an early ABC fitted with a fore and aft engine, obviously took it very seriously. He has had streamlining attached to his rear before starting a record-breaking attempt in January 1914.

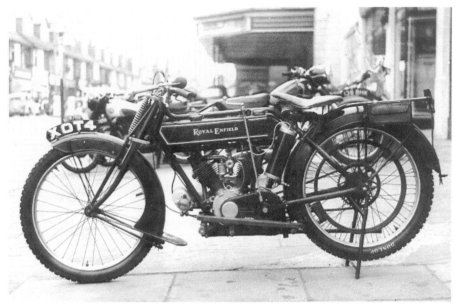

Royal Enfield made a name for themselves with their smaller capacity vee-twins, one of which finished third in the 1914 Junior TT ridden by F. J. Walker. Gear changing was effected by turning the 'tram driver's handle' on the left-hand side of the petrol tank. Unusually, the oil tank is made of glass, easy to break but having the advantage of showing the level of its oil content.

stroke made in 1912, had been superseded by a single cylinder 269 cc two-stroke. For more than fifty years Villiers Engineering specialised in this type of engine, to supply their engines to the trade and become the equivalent of JAP in the two-stroke world.

The most noticeable trend was the lowering of the riding position, so that the rider was seated in, rather than on, the machine. By bending the top tube of the frame at its rearmost end, so that it abutted the lower tank rail, the pillar-mounted saddle could be lowered considerably. Not only was the rider now seated more comfortably but he could also place both feet firmly on the ground.

In motorcycle racing there was now a reverse flow of British competitors to the Continent, to ride in various Grands Prix and offer a serious challenge. This was short-lived, as on 2nd August 1914 Britain was at war with Germany and all such activities ceased.

As the war approached, it had become obvious that the motorcycle would play an important role; there had been army ob-

servers at the 1912 TT and a campaign to enlist motorcyclists in the Territorial Army. When the war started, civilian motorcycles were commandeered, but as this proved ineffective the War Office placed substantial orders with some of the major manufacturers, especially Douglas and Triumph. Douglas responded with what was virtually their standard production model, but Triumph came out with their famous Model H early in 1915, which featured a Sturmey Archer three-speed countershaft gearbox, a kickstarter for the first time, and chain-cum-belt drive. Both the Douglas and the Triumph acquitted themselves admirably in the mud and devastation of Flanders, aided by a few other makes such as P & M (for the Royal Flying Corps), and Royal Enfield, Scott and Clyno as machine-gun carriers.

In the eyes of latter-day motorcyclists, the qualifying period for a veteran motorcycle ends on 31st December 1914, although the manufacture of motorcycles for the civilian market had been allowed to continue until 15th February 1917.

One of the toughest annual events in the sporting calendar was the Auto Cycle Union's Six Days Trial, which started from various centres in Britain. Hugh Gibson, another man associated with early Land's End to John O'Groats record-breaking attempts, ends one of the best climbs of Litton Slack with a 744 cc Clyno sidecar outfit during the 1914 event. Rain would have made the hill's stony surface treacherous.

The Scott Engineering Company Ltd, of Shipley, West Yorkshire, supplied a number of machine-gun outfits such as these. Their water-cooled twin-cylinder two-stroke engines were susceptible to freezing up under active service in winter unless the correct strength of anti-freeze had been added. Alfred Scott was inspired to design a more satisfactory three-wheel gun car to serve the same purpose, but his design was never accepted by the War Office.

Two weary despatch riders pause a while with their Douglas twins by a ruined building. It seems remarkable that these frail-looking machines could withstand such rough usage and still give reliable service after negotiating the treacherous mud of the Somme and the innumerable shell holes and bomb craters of the battlefield. The machine in the foreground has already shed its front mudguard.

An interest in restoring and riding veteran motorcycles lives on, largely through the efforts of the Sunbeam and Vintage Motor Cycle Clubs. The highlight of the year is the annual Pioneer Run from Tattenham Corner, Surrey, to Brighton, organised by the Sunbeam MCC. This photograph was taken during the concluding stage of the 1962 Run, at the seafront finish along Madeira Drive. Seen are a 1912 Triumph, a 1912 Hobart, a 1913 Humber and a 1914 Ariel.

FURTHER READING AND CLUBS

There are no books currently in print that relate exclusively to veteran motorcycles. However, a few books about old motorcycles have been written on a broader aspect, almost all in the past and no longer in print, which have become collectors' items. As they can sometimes be found for sale at autojumbles, motorcycle exhibitions and book fairs, their bibliographical details are as follows:

Clew, Jeff. *The Restoration of Vintage and Thoroughbred Motorcycles*. Haynes, 1976.
Hough, Richard, and Setright, L. J. K. *A History of the World's Motorcycles*. Allen & Unwin, 1966.
'Ixion'. *Motor Cycle Reminiscences*. Iliffe, c.1921.
'Ixion'. *Further Motor Cycle Reminiscences*. Iliffe, c.1927.
'Ixion'. *Motor Cycle Cavalcade*. Iliffe, 1950.
Setright, L. J. K. *Twistgrip*. Allen & Unwin, 1969.
Sheldon, James. *Veteran and Vintage Motor Cycles*. Batsford,1961.
Various. *The History of Motorcycling*. Orbis, 1979.
Walford, Eric W. *Early Days in the British Motor Cycle Industry*. The British Cycle and Motor Cycle Manufacturers and Traders Union, undated.

There are also a number of marque histories about individual makes of motorcycle, available from publishers such as Aston, Crowood, Haynes, and Osprey.

MAGAZINES
There is no publication that deals specifically with veteran motorcycles. The following titles do, however, often carry articles on pre-1915 machines, (as does *The Vintage Motor Cycle*, which is available only to *bona fide* members of the Vintage Motor Cycle Club).

British Bike Magazine, PO Box 19, Cowbridge, South Glamorgan CF7 7YD.
(The) Classic Motor Cycle, Bushfield House, Orton Centre, Peterborough, Cambridge-shire PE2 5UW.
Classic Motorcycling Legends, 80 Kingsway East, Dundee, Angus DD4 8SL.
Old Bike, Clayside Barn, Alstonefield, near Ashbourne, Derbyshire DE6 0AA.
Old Bike Mart, PO Box 99, Horncastle, Lincolnshire LN9 6LZ.

CLUBS
The Association of Pioneer Motor Cyclists, Heatherbank, May Close, Liphook Road, Headley, Bordon, Hampshire GU35 8LR.
The Sunbeam Motor Cycle Club, 18 Chieveley Drive, Tunbridge Wells, Kent TN2 5HQ. (Maintains the Register of Pioneer Motorcycles and certifies *bona fide* veteran machines; also the organising body of the annual Pioneer Run.)
The Vintage Motor Cycle Club Ltd, Allen House, Wetmore Road, Burton-upon-Trent, Staffordshire DE14 1SN. (Interest extends to cover all motorcycles more than twenty-five years old, including veterans.)

PLACES TO VISIT

Intending visitors are advised to find out times of opening and to ascertain that items of interest will be on display before making a special journey.

Birmingham Museum of Science and Industry, Newhall Street, Birmingham, West Midlands B3 1RZ. Telephone: 0121-235 1661.
Haynes Motor Museum, Sparkford, near Yeovil, Somerset BA22 7LF. Telephone: 01963 440804.
National Motor Museum, John Montagu Building, Beaulieu, Brockenhurst, Hampshire SO42 7ZN. Telephone: 01590 612345.
National Motorcycle Museum, Coventry Road, Bickenhall, Solihull, West Midlands B92 0EJ. Telephone: 01675 443311.
The Sammy Miller Museum, Gore Road, New Milton, Hampshire BH25 6TF. Telephone: 01425 619696.
Science Museum, Exhibition Road, South Kensington, London SW7 2DD. Telephone: 0171-938 8000.
Science Museum, Red Barn Gate, Wroughton, near Swindon, Wiltshire SN4 9NS. Telephone: 01793 814466
Stanford Hall Motorcycle Museum, Stanford Hall, Lutterworth, Leicestershire LE17 6DH. Telephone: 01788 860250.

Harry Bashall, one of three brothers who raced motorcycles, had most of his racing successes with BAT, but he decided he would have a better chance with a Douglas than with the Humber he had elected to ride in the 1912 Junior Race. He was right, as his Douglas finished in first place. The resultant publicity helped Douglas secure a War Department contract for the supply of machines during the First World War. He is seen here with a vee-twin BAT and sidecar at Brooklands in 1913.